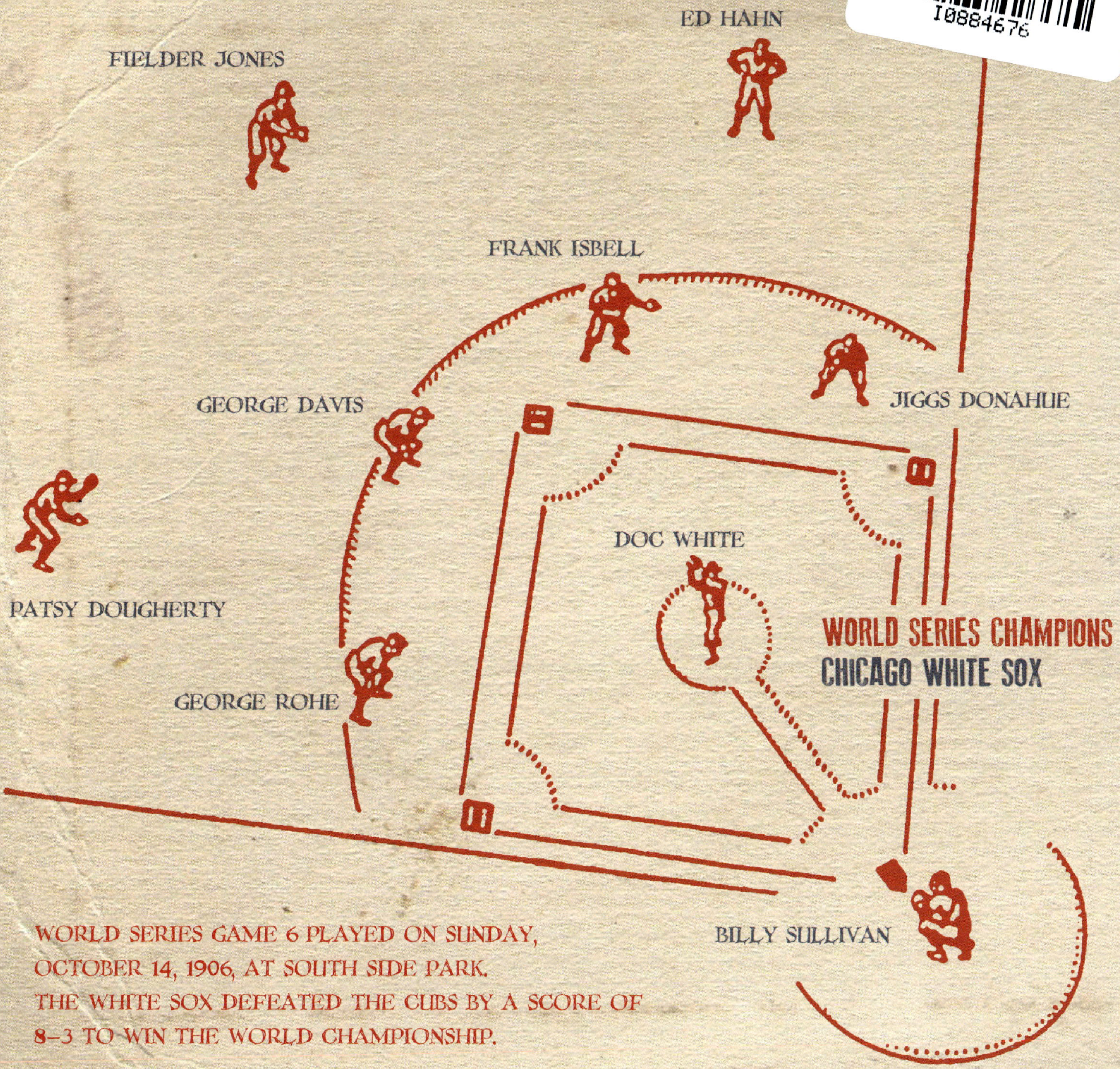

WORLD SERIES GAME 6 PLAYED ON SUNDAY, OCTOBER 14, 1906, AT SOUTH SIDE PARK. THE WHITE SOX DEFEATED THE CUBS BY A SCORE OF 8–3 TO WIN THE WORLD CHAMPIONSHIP.

SOX

WORLD SERIES CHAMPIONS

CHICAGO WHITE SOX

SARA GILBERT

CREATIVE PAPERBACKS

Published by Creative Paperbacks
P.O. Box 227, Mankato, Minnesota 56002
Creative Paperbacks is an imprint of The Creative Company
www.thecreativecompany.us

Design and production by Blue Design (www.bluedes.com)
Art direction by Rita Marshall
Printed in the United States of America

Photographs by Corbis (Bettmann), Getty Images (David Banks, Mark Carnishaw/MLB Photos, Chicago History Museum/Archive Photos, Jonathan Daniel, Focus On Sport, Otto Greule Jr, Bruce Kluckhohn/MLB Photos, Saul Loeb/AFP, Brad Mangin/MLB Photos, Jim McIsaac, Martin D. McReynolds, Francis Miller/Time & Life Pictures, National Baseball Hall of Fame Library/MLB Photos, Scott Olson, Rich Pilling/MLB Photos, Rogers Photo Archive, Mark Rucker/Transcendental Graphics, Herb Scharfman/Sports Imagery, Donald F. Smith/Time & Life Pictures, James Squire, Ron Vesely/MLB Photos)

Library of Congress Cataloging-in-Publication Data
Gilbert, Sara.
Chicago White Sox / Sara Gilbert.
p. cm. — (World series champions)
Includes bibliographical references and index.
Summary: A simple introduction to the Chicago White Sox major league baseball team, including its start in 1900, its World Series triumphs, and its stars throughout the years.
ISBN 978-1-60818-262-6 (hardcover)
ISBN 978-0-89812-813-0 (pbk)
1. Chicago White Sox (Baseball team)—History—Juvenile literature.
I. Title.
GV875.C58G55 2013
796.357'640977311—dc23 2011051189

First edition
9 8 7 6 5 4 3 2 1

Cover: First baseman Paul Konerko
Page 2: Catcher Carlton Fisk
Page 3: Infielder Geoff Blum
Right: The White Sox's old stadium

COMISKEY PARK
HOME OF THE WHITE SOX
BOXES-GRAND STAND
BOXES-GRAND STAND
BOXES-GRAND STAND

LF
RON KITTLE

RF
JOE JACKSON

SS
LUKE APPLING

CF
JIM LANDIS

3B
ROBIN VENTURA

M
AL LOPEZ

TABLE OF CONTENTS

CHICAGO AND U.S. CELLULAR FIELD

Chicago is a big city in Illinois. It is nicknamed the "Windy City." Chicago has a ballpark called U.S. Cellular Field. A baseball team named the White Sox plays its home games there.

RIVALS AND COLORS

The White Sox are a major league baseball team. All major-league teams try to win the World Series and become world champions. The White Sox wear black-and-white uniforms. They play some of their most exciting games against their **RIVALS**, the Minnesota Twins and the Chicago Cubs.

SECOND BASEMAN GORDON BECKHAM

PITCHER TED LYONS

WHITE SOX HISTORY

The White Sox played their first season in 1901. Five years later, they faced the Cubs in the World Series. The White Sox won. In 1917, they won the world championship again!

After losing the 1919 World Series, the White Sox went into a **SLUMP** that lasted 40 years. In 1959, second baseman Nellie Fox helped the

1919 WHITE SOX

P
EARLY WYNN

C
A. J. PIERZYNSKI

3B
JOE CREDE

1B
DICK ALLEN

P
ED WALSH

LF
MINNIE MINOSO

HAROLD BAINES

team get to the World Series. But the Sox lost again.

Chicago was not as good after that. In 1970, the White Sox lost 106 games. But in 1983, hard-hitting outfielder Harold Baines helped Chicago win 99 games. The White Sox finally made the **PLAYOFFS**, but they could not get to the World Series.

PAUL KONERKO

In 2000, the White Sox started winning more often. In 2005, first baseman Paul Konerko led the team to the World Series. Chicago won by beating the Houston Astros in four straight games!

PITCHER JACK McDOWELL

"SHOELESS" JOE JACKSON

FIELDER JONES

WHITE SOX STARS

Fielder Jones was an outfielder and manager for the White Sox during their earliest seasons. He helped the Sox get to the 1906 World Series. Outfielder "Shoeless" Joe Jackson was the star of the 1917 championship team.

Big first baseman Frank Thomas played 16 seasons in Chicago. He hit 448 home runs for the White Sox. A. J. Pierzynski was a smart catcher for Chicago. Fans loved how hard he played.

Outfielder Alex Rios slammed 21 homers in 2010. He helped Chicago almost make the playoffs. With Rios smashing the ball, White Sox fans believed the team could win another world championship soon!

FRANK THOMAS

ALEX RIOS

CENTER FIELDER JUAN PIERRE

HOW THE WHITE SOX GOT THEIR NAME

The White Sox's name came from the team's uniforms. The players wore white socks, so the team was known as the White Stockings. A Chicago newspaper shortened that to White Sox. It was easier to write and to use in headlines. The new name stuck!

ABOUT THE WHITE SOX

First season: 1901

League/division: American League, Central Division

World Series championships:

1906 *4 games to 2 versus Chicago Cubs*

1917 *4 games to 2 versus New York Giants*

2005 *4 games to 0 versus Houston Astros*

White Sox Web site for kids:

http://mlb.mlb.com/mlb/kids/index.jsp?c_id=cws

Club MLB:

http://web.clubmlb.com/index.html

GLOSSARY

PLAYOFFS — all the games (including the World Series) after the regular season that are played to decide who the champion will be

RIVALS — teams that play extra hard against each other

SLUMP — a period of time when a team loses more games than it wins

INDEX